POETRY IS DEAD

A poetry collection by O.B. Thompson

2nd Edition

o.b.
thompson

Published by WarmBreeze Digital Publishing

Contents

Authors Notes

The thing that has struck me the most about re-releasing the newest versions of my books is that the authors notes could largely have been written in the present day, instead of at the time of release. Nothing ever truly changes.

A quote that I did enjoy from the original notes for this collection was from Cyril Connolly, who wrote that it was "better to write for yourself with no public, than for the public with no self." I still truly believe that, which is why another quote that I found amusing from the original notes was that "no one cares that much about poetry anymore". That was me. I wrote that. And it turned out to be remarkably prescient as it goes because I too fell out of love with poetry and have only just started to pick up the pen once more.

In doing so, I started to write as a method of attempting to heal and make sense of my life. As a writer without a public, I can relate more to this quote than anything else I've ever heard. It also has the smallest hint of irony that I am now releasing these collections again, purely with the intent to try and grow my audience and public. Perhaps I am a hypocrite, or perhaps I'm just bored.

Another thing that hasn't changed though is my faith in this body of work. I don't particularly enjoy reading my own work but I feel confident enough to say that I believe this holds up as a preservation of memories, people and times that have long gone from my life.

And even though you weren't there to experience these things directly, I hope that you can live through my words and embrace the emotion with which they were written.

LIFE IS A HELL OF A THING TO HAPPEN TO A PERSON.

David Rossi

The Sound of Music

From angels lips comes her heavenly call;
Impossible to resist;
It glides in the night,
And settles softly on my humbled ear.
Whisks me off my listless feet,
And forward to her arms.

A thousand tiny harps,
Play ballads in my captivated heart.
Her resonance strikes fear,
In the hearts of misunderstanding men
But caresses the souls of those tragic few held dear.

A wave carries me to sea,
As her forgiving voice washes over me.

Purple Haze

My purple vision haunts the lonely nights;
Stirring quietly,
Moving briskly,
A wondrous lust takes hold.

Butterflies begin to rise,
She stalks the night of which she hunts.

A perfect vision of a beautiful trap,
She takes me quietly within her jaws,
The silent night is no more.

Enticed.
Entrapped.

I am servant nor master
We are one in the same
Take this night slow, my love,
It may never come again.

Shining Example

The night shines on her
Soft, elegant beauty;
Moves freely in the night;
Eyes aglow;
Heart beating to a different rhythm.

Battle cries echo on secretive fortress walls;
Hands grip tightly to love's salvation;
Piercing eyes tell their own tale;

No more anger, betrayal or fear;
Chin up, my love
It only gets better from here.

A solitary kiss
Spills a thousand words into yearning ears,
And hungry mouths swallow them whole.

Love is not a matter of the body but of the mind;
It can be cruel, painful,
But sometimes kind.

Unwittingly it could take years to find,
And sometimes you will be wise;
To look right before your disbelieving eyes.

Mountain Lion

Hear the call of the ravenous mountain lions,
On the famous hills,
I come from far and wide to make my devotion;
To the pillars of my satisfaction.

Contemplative views fill me with pleasure,
The succulent taste of fresh crisp air soothes my aching
lungs,
A mountain lion roars,
I climb the hill again.

A Souvenir

Tender magnificence,
Holds the key to a thousand smiles.

Hands shake,
Bodies ache,
For the simple caress.

Poetry in motion,
Does no justice to perfect form,
Just as disbelievers do no justice to themselves.

Behold the beauty ten thousand sonnets cannot explain;
This is no sonnet my dear,
Just a love letter; a souvenir.

Of everything we have;
Of everything we had;
Of everything I lost.

Identity Card

On that old marble floor;
I found a key,
Used no more.
The key to my heart
Is rusted and forgotten;
As it was from the start.

Last time that I gave it away,
It ended up here;
On that old marble floor;
From now on I'll keep it near.

Learn from my mistake;
Hold yourself in high regard;
Keep your heart to yourself;
Your very own identity card.

07:34 a.m.

Woke up with a smile upon my face,
For the first time in a while.
The heat's died down upon us,
With nobody staring,
Criticizing every move we make,
And yet I still can't seem to beat this sinking feeling.

10:16 p.m.

It took me all day,
To write one fucking haiku,
Now I cannot stop.

1:32 a.m.

Here I sit by the window,
On this cold lonely night,
With my hand down my pants;
Looking out below at
All the people scurrying like ants.

3:05 a.m.

Fighting with sleep,
Never brought me much peace.
Should I try counting sheep?
Or maybe count geese?

What's the point?
I can't sleep.

Torches and Pitchforks

You lied one too many times,
The mob is on its way,
Torches and pitchforks at the ready;
Can something be your fault,
If you're only partly to blame?

They'll take you dead or alive,
You'll be famous,
For your heinous crimes against your own country,
Seek asylum south;
Because here you won't survive.

Declaration

I declare war on the world.

The entire human race,
The ones I've come to hate;
Who I'll stop at nothing to annihilate.

Time is going backwards;
I'm the only one who's thinking forwards;
It's nature versus nurture;
And we all know existence is torture;
So let's start the slaughter.

This world holds nothing as far as I can see;
Everyone walks around like the world owes them everything
for free,
But you are nothing you see,
I've made you everything you can and will be.

So how can it be that existence ends with me?

Indictment

Selfie loving teens breeding uneducated fiends;
A generation of failure;
Breeds another generation governed by disgusting behaviour;
Kids out with more guns than an arsenal;
Our streets have turned farcical.
Here we are waiting,
For a legally clean cardinal,
To return order to the anarchical.

Fill a head with knowledge; not a bullet;
And acknowledge that there is a way out.

Life isn't a movie,
Life is a duty,
A cross we all must bear,
So why not make it fair?

Modern life is fucked;
And there's nothing I can do.

Modern life is fucked;
I could help but I really don't want to.

Terror on the Shores

I've got a feeling I've been lied to by the media,
And that video games and music;
Are not the cause of my hysteria.

I'm a product of my environment;
Nothing more, nothing less;
Than a servant to this tyrant;
That I see destroying the press.
The ones who try to oppress,
Those who refuse to tow the line.

While they tell us everything's fine;
Like a sadistic nursery rhyme;
They think the worlds gone blind,
But we're more awake than ever.

Your reign of terror can't last forever.

Title Censored

My life is in a state of perpetual motion,
A deadly cocktail of too much ineffectual emotion.

Even though these words I write they may seem intellectual;
One day they will be banned,
I know that is inevitable,
And my friend; that is regrettable.

Opulence

We live in the age of reason,
Yet knowledge swallows us whole,
We're collapsing under the force of the black tide,
Commercial arrogance is leprosy eating us alive.

We bow to the banker;
And we jail the thinker;
The end of days is nigh.

We will end in fire,
A selfish flame flickers,
We will end in their opulence.

Slaves to the rich;
Impoverished, alone
Scared.

Fear and Loathing

We speak in fear;
What good is a world where even the journalists cower?

It's the fault of the ninety nine per cent;
For not standing up and speaking without consent;
There's no need to reinvent the past or the present.

Only to speak the truth,
And turn general ignorance to general sentience,
So that I can finish my sentence without a gasp or a shriek.
"Can he say that?"
"Of course he can, let the man speak!"

Fly Away

Disenchanted constituents from broken homes,
Run rampant in the streets creating mindless violence,
As a method of disassembling government sponsored silence.

The eagle rules with an iron fist;
His rubber bullets are toys;
Presents for who try to resist;
He laughs at everything he destroys.

The uncensored populace,
Fly south for the winter,
And spread your wings,
Free speech is now a splinter;
Under the thumb of false kings.

Freedom fighters on an unseen battlefield,
Hunting the eagle for all he's concealed,
And all that's now illegal.

When he's caught,
His neck will snap,
Like a promise of prosperity,
And it will end this senseless scrap.

Flap,
Flap.

Snap,
Snap.

Identity Fraud

Where is our democracy? It's gone, replaced.
By a financial meritocracy;
And the profligacy of this downright hypocrisy,
Is burning my eyes like a girl who just opened the front door.
The world I knew isn't here anymore;
Whether you are rich or poor.

I feel so fucking distraught;
That there can be so much food for thought,
While there's people starving,
In countries whose bank balance reads below nought.
Because of the land we've raped and pillaged;
For oil we should have just bought.

Yet they take and they take;
When there's people struggling here in the land you hold
dear;
And for what? A cheaper pair of shoes?

This is what happens when the government choose to kill,
In the name of a God who's gone and left,
Because he was appalled at what you'd done in his name,
Now my life has become some type of identity fraud.

And I want my fucking money back.

On Nature

Man by nature is timid,
Afraid of what he does not understand,
What he cannot understand,
What he cannot understand about himself.

Women by nature are not timid,
A woman's heart more accepting,
More human somehow,
She frightens man with power;
Oh, how they cower.

> I stand aside and laugh
> At the crying misogynist.

System Failure

How can you oppress the way that a woman wants to dress?
Because of a sick freak who says she deserved it?

When I hear words like that,
Our future seems bleak,
How can you have such cheek?
To spout crap like that,
It doesn't make you look innocent,
It makes you look weak.

Recep

The self-important man makes the greatest fool,
For he has no failings,
And the mirror never lies,
He is blind from staring into the sun.

The self-important man can never be trusted,
A trivial life glorified by fear,
Some things are not as they appear,
Robbed blind by impotence,
Logic and reason gives way to narcissistic importance;
On his self-fulfilling judgment day.

Fixed on his own insecurities,
A complex persuasion with endless possibilities;
Fed this ruthless invasion of disregarded privacy;
Destroying his own democracy;
To hide secrets that could bring a country down.

Sickening.

Blind Eye

Six million people persecuted and murdered,
I sit here and hear someone say they probably deserved it?
I feel sick inside.

Who are you to decide who should have lived and who died?

They say general ignorance is bliss,
If that's the case then we face the abyss,
What kind of imbecile could so easily dismiss,
This cataclysmic event that scarred the course of history
But I guess we could talk about something else instead.

Box of Snakes

A box of snakes is what you make of it,
Could be used for good or evil,
For your wealth or for your giving,
That's completely your decision.

If you try to rid of them,
They'll just come back to bite you.
Do not play with fire;
Or you'll end up getting burnt.

Arrogance

Is it not a dream that conquers us?
A thoughtless portal into your sub-conscience,
This audacious attempt at freedom is consuming reality,
And destroying all you hold dear.

Your skin will writhe in pain,
And the lepers thrive to feast upon your rotting skin,
Only one can save you from this mortal sin,
But when it all goes wrong,
You just blame it on Him.

Commodity

A game controlled by money is no longer a game,
It's a toy.

A toy is not real,
A toy has no emotion,
A toy has no feeling.

If you play too much with a toy; it will break and it will
crumble.

Irreplaceable,
Unfixable,
Unlovable.

We are not the play things of the rich;
We are not customers to be charmed or objects to be sold;
We are people;
We are fans;
And we are angry.

Do not take away our love;
Do not take away our game;
Because when it all goes wrong for you,
And trust me, soon it will,
You'll have no one left to blame.

Tiger

A tiger on a
Mountain rarely smiles for
He can see it all.

Turned to Stone

Hear the swirling roar,
It breaks early morning silence,
The night is no more,
Broken by narcissistic footsteps on lazy stone,
And troubled mortar.

How they moan in displeasure,
At being used in such a way,
A life so unpleasant serves a greater purpose;
And fills a greater canvas.

He grumbles in anger,
But there's nothing he can do.

Dead End Path

Tired heads speak clearer than ever,
Weary eyes and troubled minds,
Scream loudly through the wind.

Hungry,
Alone,
Contemplative.

The condition of all young men trying to find their way in the
world.

Many paths fascinate,
But dead ends block the way.

In the end it matters not what you choose to do;
Because when the bell tolls,
The rich will be as dead as me and you.

Crows

On tenterhooks and crumbling floors,
We walk silently to the mortal grave.
The crow stands watch on heavens hellish gates;
Looking down on us,
Lying in wait,
For us to join him one day.

When our time comes we all run and hide,
Never ready to leave the world behind;
What must the crow think? Sat way up there,
He must be lonely and the world doesn't care.

Hurricanes and Earthquakes

The floor shakes beneath our feet,
Telemetry off the chart,
The damage uncontrollable,
Loss of life severe,
All that becomes clear,
No one can survive here,
And now we can't evacuate,
The rest is up to fate.

They told us it was coming,
Yet you sat and nothing,
Up there in your own fortress,
Of ignorance and disdain.
No water, not a drop, shall pass
Your impenetrable wall.

But be careful now,
Look at the sky;
The eye of the storm is on its way.

Arguing with God

The truth is, it isn't pretty, beautiful or handsome;
It's ugly, like me;
Don't believe me? Come and see.

Sometimes I think about slitting my wrist and ending it all;
Just to see how far my blood shoots up the wall;
It'll be like Jackson Pollock on an acid trip;
Maybe I'll meet God to find out if he exists;
So he can settle all the ethical conflicts,
In my head about taking another man to bed.

I mean, I might as well ask.

Because this argument persists,
We all know how stupid it is,
It's my body and his is his.

Lest Ye Be Judged

Blank stares on grey faces,
Look up to the sky;
And pray,
"Will you save us all today?"
Look and laugh,
In smug condescension,
Nobody is coming soon.

When looking up is all you know;
It becomes harder to let go;
Of everything you once believed;
In place of something new;
But know that nothing's new;
Especially you.

Drawing Blanks

Heartbeat racing;
Throbbing veins;
Drenched in sweat;
The fear takes over.

Time is going slower but the world beings to spin;
Red mist descends over silent ridges,
Eyes roll and tongues wag,
Lights flicker on and off,
Blood is in the air.

Faint.
Fall.
The only truth is in our veins.

Classic Signs of Ageing

The mood once more is sombre;
The air is filled with hatred,
Befouling every night.

I'm caught in solitary moments;
Of remembering that I'm human;
Our suffering and the plight.

This what we are;
It is what we have become.

We are aware of what we are;
We know what's coming next.

This is a classic sign of ageing;
The whole world is burning slowly;
We are the only warriors;
And our time is rapidly fading.

Dockyard

Swaying in a sympathetic wind;
Rusted homes of former glory;
Sit lonely on the shore,
Their hero's stories heard no more.

Ramblings of an Inuit

A frozen wasteland so beautiful;
Paint upon the blank canvas;
The finest gift of all.
Look out for miles,
The twinkle of the snow,
Lights up all the humble smiles.

Night is closer than day,
Sky alight with eyes,
That capture a thousand wanderers;
In awe of something special,

The ice desert stands alone,
And brings us all to tears,
Magnifying the intensity,
Of the brilliant daylight,
Illuminating fields of white,
And sea of blue.

A Reflection

Chocolate brothels on streets of common vice;
Lead each dreary eyed man;
Stumbling down paths of sloth and gluttony;
For we are all willing victims here;
A timid love affair with the richer things in life;
I will never be the same again.

The city has no secrets;
Holds no trembling fear;
A simple place that lives so quietly,
It comes alive under light;
And through the biting cold;
Although the cold trials me;
There is no question;
That this is where I want to be;
In this grand, old city.

Semper Invicta

A beautiful city,
Haunted by memories of blood and loss,
New life towers high above the old,
Into the sky.

Hear the melodies of Chopin;
That the softest angels sing;
Here in Warsaw, hope is king;
In the city that never dies.

Market Town

Hustling,
Bustling,
Food papers rustling.

The invading air is oh so pleasant;
Heaven scent,
By Ambrosia's fair hand.
Travel stall to stall,
Life's simple pleasures call,
Out to a starving wanderer.

Take your pick;
It's easy to get lost in it.

The mind flows like wine,
As my lips begin to purse, my feet carry me home;
That first taste; utterly divine.

How can it be;
That in a city almost devoid of pleasure;
Its finest hidden simple treasure;
Lies not in a famous cathedral, abbey or shop?
Instead it's underneath a simple bridge,
That the world does stop.

One Early Morning

A thin veil covers the glistening horizon,
Tumultuous landscape frail in the early light,
Cold air penetrated by the warm sun,
Peeking its head in trepidation through dusty morning clouds.

The luminous technicolor sky,
Lights the gloomy path with three colours at once;
The fiery black lights the way;
Brilliant orange fights back.

A deathly blue lingers,
Natural light so artificial on this perfect day.

Down pours the rain,
Treading lightly on the gentle ebb of the twinkling river;
Swaying in the gentle wind,
Here comes the fearsome sky again.

The King of Belgium

Golden throws on threads divine;
A blend so precious,
This treasure of mine.

The glimmer of your hair;
Matches the beautiful décor,
Which with the world I shall not share.

For we're nothing to all we see;
But in our perfect world,
We live in luxury.

Grote Markt

Winding cobbles filled with excitement and flowing with
beer;
Lead to that majestic place,
Alive with colour buoyant with murmurs,
About the magnificence of those ancient towers,
Watching down on us all;
Smiling.

This is the only place to be.

British Summer Time

Summer walks on fresh shores,
Greet the new light,
Revelling in the gentle flight;
Of a thousand birds,
Dance to the echo,
Of an ocean's thunderous roar.

Children play so merrily,
On the pebbled beach,
Oblivious to the world,
And here I sit,
Much closer to the world,
Than I could ever admit.

The Cafe

Winding roads of bliss,
Temples of the soul,
Feast the senses.

The sights bathed in the glorious lights,
The smells,
And their enchanting spells;
The sounds,
Of eager feet on medieval grounds.

Shops cling together,
Vendors wail,
Patrons bustle,
Sit by the roadside and let the world pass by.

What'll it be sir?
"Café-Vermouth"
And one for the lady too.

Grand Old Lady

Deafening drums roll and heads go silent;
No thoughts needed,
Just the fear;
The expectation;
The deadly anticipation.

Nerves are shredded,
Stomachs tight,
The drum roll ends,
It's time to fight.

A hero's welcome;
A villain's snarl;
The street roars,
Expectation gone,
It's time to play,

Game on.

The English Way

Nervous eyes catch a glance;
Across the crowded plain;
We're just two simple strangers waiting for a train.

The battle looms as our chariot beckons;
The war is won in those vital seconds;
Shaking madly side to side;
Apologising awkwardly as our bodies collide.

Steel on steel,
Flesh on flesh.

The calming sound,
Of being caught in a jungle,
On the London Underground.

Fields of Kent

The red mist descends;
No one knows where it ends.

But the sky is grey;
As this gentle day comes crashing into view;
The silent rolling hills pass on the haunting chills,
Birds cry out;
In hopeful doubt;
The day begins again.

Flowers perk and raise their heads;
A whirlpool of powerful blues and brilliant reds.

Picture perfect scenery;
Holds lust and powerful mystery.

All aglow in mid-morning sun,
The humble fields of England;
A green and mighty kingdom;
Sit silently tonight,
Precious in the fading light.

Another day has ended.

Old Wien

Up here;
So peaceful above the world,
Watching the city,
As it unfurled beneath my feet.

On the horizon;
I see the sunset borders far and wide,
Where Heaven and Earth collide,
Reach out and touch God as he looks down on this fair city.

This is His country;
For so long I struggled;
But now he's coming back to me again,
Thanks to old Wien.

Waterways

The deep winding alleys of ancient times,
Whisper secret tongues to lovers.
The Venice of Flanders stirs in the silent night;
Inhale her beauty.

A cacophony of the senses;
Bring humble men to their knees.
In a town so quaint,
Beneath the world,
It's here we wait;
To be rescued from this pleasant hell.

Where the Mountains Meet the Sea

Beating sun warms my humble skin;
The brilliant daylight falls down upon its garden;
Rays filled with muse caress a lonely traveller;
Luscious mountains stand proud looking down on a vibrant metropolis;
Inflicting awe and wonder on simple humble patrons.
Crisp air breathes life into tired lives;
Crunching sand stands firm beneath exhausted feet;
Jagged coasts impeccable.

The freedom,
White and blue;
Gaze upon their splendour,
For me it's nothing new.
Suburban jungles collide with dense fields of brown and green;
City sounds fill the ears,
People dance to their powerful rhythm,
They come alive in summer.

No division or unity;
Protected by their brother,
Standing tall,
High in the trees away from it all;
Take heavens ascent and meet the royal call.

Crusaders come from all around to see this famous bay of dreams;
Where the mountains meet the sea.

Days End

On modern streets of ancient times,
We walk gently,
Through our simple lives.

We're not alone,
Dusty windows offer portals into secrecy;
Another world lies beyond;
The last charade of privacy.

Slanting roads to hidden treasures,
A town of fools;
Hides simple pleasures.

Dig up the roots of any man and you will find,
Something he can never leave behind.

This ghastly town clings to me;
In my shame,
For all to see.

But sitting by the waterside,
Staring out into the vast temptation of the sea;
I get the feeling,
That nowhere can ever mean as much,
As this place does to me.

Montmartre

Down the rolling hills;
Cobbled streets bathe in cold artificial glow,
Thinly leafed trees,
Barely covers a busker's lonely song.

Twisting cafes harbour poet's dreams,
Artistic souls are destined to go unnoticed here it seems;
The views are stunning;
Salesman cunning.

The beating heart of Paris stirs,
Nothing ordinary occurs in this gentle lovers quarter;
Lose yourself to find yourself,
On the mount of rolling hills.

In Critique

Picturesque but fading,
A crumbling ruin;
Holds faint hopes of rejuvenation;
Estranged awards and prizes offer little compensation.

For this ghost of a city,
Haunted by false glory,
Scarred by its own vanity,
Lays destined for dormancy.

Not asleep but comatose,
How Arnold would wince,
If the cities famous prince,
Could see you now.

Sitting in London

The clatter of hooves,
Disturbs the peaceful ambience;
Of this pleasant day.
  My concrete chair,
  Is fair game;
  To busy passing souls.

Prater

As I watch the lights,
Swirl out through the dark,
Upon the Sandman's quest;
I do embark,
As I look out upon,
Old Prater Park.

A swirling dream takes hold;
I dream of those colours;
Faded blue and dazzling gold;
And with sluggish lark,
I look out in joy upon,
Old Prater Park.

The Night Train to Rangoon

Dreary eyes flicker under the gentle rushing light;
Heads drift away,
And the train marches into the night.

Chariots of steel on polished rails carry us home;
The tip-tapping of children's fingers on wooden seats;
Distract the last weary eyes from closing.

An unassuming whistle rouses fallen eyes,
Before they drift away again;
I, for one, cannot sleep tonight.

The dusty window holds my gaze;
Staring out over the lonely midnight landscape,
Contemplating the existence of this never ending world.

As I began to wonder for the thousandth time;
A sound begins to catch my ear;

Tip
Tap
Tip
Tap

My thoughts are lost inside my head, never to be found;
At least for now, this train is homeward bound.

City of Pride

A city by the river,
Living so proud;
To the glory of music,
A blessing endowed.

In from the cold,
Boats sail in ancient ports;
A city united by grief,
Divided by sports.

A heated rivalry,
In colours red or blue;
Defines a city,
Where the liver bird flew.

The Bear Pit

The bloody pit beckons;
A foul stench of death haunts the tainted air;
Terror reigns on the so-called golden fields;
Blood diamonds stolen by the undeserving;
The only blood spilt is that which is replaceable.

Outside the pit is organised hell;
Inside the pit is heavenly carnage;
Introverted personalities intimidate my captors;
But they do not intimidate me.

I am hunted, I am free.

The Hunted

It seems, for great shame
That life is passing me by;
"Oh life, thou art failing me."

We live in hypocrisy of privacy,
Because we have none anymore;
Yet we hide ourselves away;
It's not just you and me,
More like everyone you see.

We are being hunted,
For what films we like;
For which music we listen to;
And which foods we eat at 2am.

If knowledge is power,
Why aren't I king?

Life isn't passing by me;
It's passing right through me.

The War

Light-headed dreams are never easy;
They taunt the lonely man,
The light makes him queasy;
But the dark makes him sick,
From the nightmares it holds.

Slumber takes its grip,
She shines through in her darkness,
He quivers,
Sun kissed skin haunted by ruby lips;
Sandy hair devastated with a crimson smile;
Burning blue eyes gladly pierce me;
Uneasy stares beckon forth,
A haunting whisper so seductive;
Bringing fond memories of a devilish nightmare.

You lay in wait for me to sleep;
My life is surrendered to a spectre;
No food passes these lips of yours;
I've surrendered to you.

I know I've seen you before,
This is not over.

[...]

The beautiful air of death hangs like a cloud,
Over this marriage bed;
Gone but never left,
The dream is over,
I'm coming for you.

Another tedious day draws to an end;
Lay down in bed and rest my eyes;
Where is my ghostly mistress tonight?
The love that I despise.
She skulks alone in the background hidden from sight;
I tell myself it's just a dream,
But that gave me such a fright.

Eyes flatter to deceive,
In a manner most unknown;
They fool me once as she speaks
In that haunted calming tone.
She glides across the dusty floor,
To whisper softly to me;
The only thing you need to know,
In your dreams I'll always be.

I awoke.

[...]

The music blares all around;
Visions of beauty dance through the night,
Dancing so gracefully to the intoxicating sound.

Tonight she wants to see me;
To stare me dead in the face;
So, running I come,
Destined for her warm embrace;
My fingers go numb,
And my heart starts to race;
My head starts to wonder,
Is this the end of the chase?

As I lean in for a kiss I see
A single tear in her eye;
She says it's for me,
Silently we cry;
Before she whispers again;
This must be goodbye.

She waves,
Before turning the saddest of turns,
It all becomes clear,
That this man never learns.

[...]

My dreams are not my own tonight;
Visions of tantalizing angel wings on golden sheets of former
anguish;
Stir this fatal sleep.

But as I rub dry eyes I find myself awake;
Outside of your control,
The fragrance of your beauty can tempt this man no more.

Staring out the window,
Overlooking the destitution that this war has brought;
A lonely figure sits,
Facing the wall,
On that frail old park bench;
Sandy hair blowing in the wind.

Ghosts

There are chains around my throat;
Forged in regret, rusted with the sands,
Not yet eroded;
Hidden in plain sight.

Twisted by the love of hate,
Suffocating the truth;
One too many times cold dead hands pull me down,
And wrap the chains around my neck;
Their fury, tight

They strangle;
Squeeze;
A vengeful bite.

When the chains come off I shall be free,
But they will still be there in spirit;
Pulling around my neck,
Dangling, in the breeze.

Dreams

When is a dream no longer a dream?
If nothing seems real and we've seen everything before.

When nothing is new and real life is a blur;
We live out a déjà vu,
Just to pass the time;
Before we all curl up and die.

It's not pleasant,
It's not pretty,
It's life.
Sleep tight.

Matador

Clear the way for the new man in town;
He holds his head high and dreams of success,
Neigh; envisions the future.

Pride emblazoned on his mighty chest;
He carries expectation on his back;
Falling upwards never looked so easy.

Smiles all around;
The grass is greener no more.
Right here;
Right now;
Is the place to be.

Let the defiant trumpets sound;
The bull charges once more;
He seems so helpless, alone
Held off with guile and wit;
By the matador unknown.

To him that visions of red;
Will give way to the visions of blue that dance in his head.

The Race

From the lifeless wreckage;
The choking engine sputters into life;

Coughing.
Purring.
Roaring.

The engine turns;
And the machine begins to roll;

Unstoppable.
Unflappable.
Untouchable.

The adrenaline is pumping,
Waiting is no more, excitement building;
Everything we've been waiting for.

King of Nowhere

Sitting by the window, you're wondering;
Why am I God's leader?

Proclaim your prophecy of sanity and reason;
Servants pin you down;
Reality beings to strike;
The pills have saved your life but they no longer work.

A bitter taste left behind
In a mouth so dry;
It burns like deadwood in the desert sun;
Pull the plug and let the king die with dignity.

You were told you are the king of nowhere;
But really, in your heart,
You are the king of everywhere.

Raymond

Urban rhythms stir the gentle soldier;
Footsteps on hollow cobbles;
Harsh stone dressed in subtle leather;
Echo around his solitary room;
Anxious dogs bark to tranquil owners;
Just another urban day to treasure.

The sun penetrates his dusty window;
Rag curtains do little to shut out intruders;
He stirs again;
The pillow is an uncomfortable mistress;
He used to love this place;
But this is now and that was then.

It used to smell like home once;
Before he was silently bitten,
By that dreadful homesick curse;
Utopia is beautiful,
And everything's the same here;
Yet somehow slightly worse.

In Earnest

Stumbling through a drunken haze;
On these lazy Parisian days;
A lonely soul;
Out for his weekly Sunday stroll;
He marauds the cobbled Latin streets;
Yearning for his mistress' sheets.

He staggers towards Saint-Sulpice;
Seeking peace,
From the voices in his mind;
Scared of what he'll find;
No peace is found;
Homeward bound.

There outside sits a lonely mirror;
Through the mist his face is clearer than it ever was before;
Paris has lost its allure;
And without doubt;
He knows he must get out.

Wanderer

Tired feet hug the cobbled path;
Dreary eyes trouble party makers;

Laughter.

Weariness takes hold and on trudges the faceless man,
Tired of life;
Haunted by the darkness in the city of light;
No room for the stranger in a city that raised him;
Held in contempt by a city that owns him;
The faceless man is tired of life.

Attired in grey;
He walks alone;
All night and all day in a city that broke him;
The faceless man is tired of life.

That all ends today;
A gin soaked anger grips like a vice;
He screams out in despair,
Not once.. but twice.

The end is coming quickly;
It's something too familiar;
Slips;
Stumbles;
Falls.

[...]

The cold cobbled path holds no solace for his old weary
head;
He will be going home tonight;
For the streets no longer shelter our weary, broken, faceless
man
From the city that stole his fight.
Where are you going tonight?
The world is so big, so wide;
There is almost nowhere to hide;
The faceless man walks alone in the night.

These are his streets,
The streets that made him hold no grudge;
He may hate a city of fallen angels but still he returns here,
Time after time;
Year after year.

The charmless wife puts out his dinner;
She knows not where he is;
No longer does she care;
The faceless man is with his mistress tonight.

She does not know the woman whose husband she stole;
A city more beautiful than he;
But with an ugly soul,
She is magnificent no more.

The Smoke

Smoke billows down,
In streams of ghastly terror,
The fire has spread,
Disaster ahead.

Tears cannot steady the vast flames;
Onlookers rush helplessly;
Smoke gets in your eyes;
Thick clouds cover helpless skies;
We shall not forget what happened here.

Years later;
On a tragic second stage;
There is still no comfort to be found,
In memoriam of the day,
That words can't fix;
The catastrophe of the fifty-six.

Tito

We find strength in the strangest places;
Sometimes in words,
Sometimes in games,
As long as we're surrounded by familiar faces.

For all to see;
We stand tall in battle,
And all take strength from you,
Our revered Marquis.

Never forget;
That our time is not set;
Not enough time with so much to do,
But most importantly,
We will never forget you.

Twenty-Five

Twenty-five years have passed;
Still we're haunted by the ghosts of the past;
But the smiles of justice are coming at last.

We shall lay them to rest,
In the wake of relentless protest;
And tears fall on banners of hope;
Because the city can cope.

With all the lies that you throw,
About that fateful day;
Twenty-five years ago.

C'est la Vie

People say that I'm miserable all the time, but I'm not.
I am happy sometimes;
It's just that when I am happy;
I don't talk to people about it because then
I would be sad again.

Dead or alive?